the doors

THE BEST OF

WISE PUBLICATIONS
London / New York / Paris / Sydney / Copenhagen / Berlin / Madrid / Tokyo

Exclusive distributors:
Music Sales Limited
14/15 Berners Street, London W1T 3LJ, England.
Music Sales Pty Limited
Units 3-4 Willfox Street, Condell Park, NSW 2200,
Australia.

Order No. AM974072
ISBN 0-7119-9423-4
This book © Copyright 2002
by Wise Publications.

Unauthorised reproduction of any part of this publication by any means including photocopying is an
infringement of copyright.

New music arrangements by Matt Cowe.
Music processed by Simon Troup.
Cover images courtesy of
Warner Music International/Elektra.
Page 112 image courtesy of LFI.

Printed and bound in the EU.

Your Guarantee of Quality:
As publishers, we strive to produce every
book to the highest commercial standards.
While endeavouring to retain the original running
order of the recorded album, the book has been
carefully designed to minimise awkward page
turns and to make playing from it a real pleasure.
Particular care has been given to specifying
acid-free, neutral-sized paper made from pulps
which have not been elemental chlorine bleached.
This pulp is from farmed sustainable forests and was
produced with special regard for the environment.
Throughout, the printing and binding have been
planned to ensure a sturdy, attractive publication
which should give years of enjoyment.
If your copy fails to meet our high standards,
please inform us and we will gladly replace it.

www.musicsales.com

Riders On The Storm

Words & Music by The Doors

© Copyright 1971 Doors Music Company, USA.
Rondor Music (London) Limited, 10A Parsons Green, London SW6 4TW for the United Kingdom and the Republic of Ireland.
All Rights Reserved. International Copyright Secured.

a long hol - i - day;   let your child -ren play.   If you
Take him by the hand;   make him un - der stand.   The

give this man a ride, sweet   fam - i - ly will die.   Kill - er on the road.   Yeah. _____
world on you de-pends, our   life will nev - er end.   Got - ta love your man.

2. Girl you

*Use Rhy. Fig. 2 as a model for improvisation throughout this section.

Ri - ders on the storm. _____ Ri - ders on the storm. ___

Light My Fire

Words & Music by The Doors

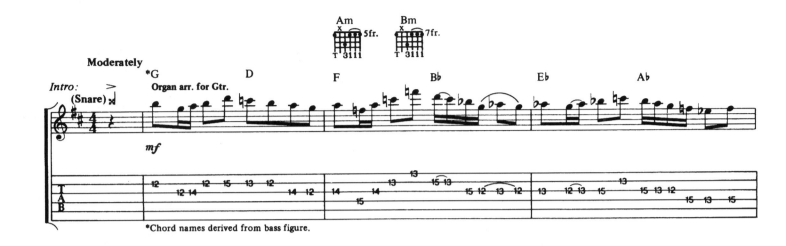

*Chord names derived from bass figure.

© Copyright 1967 Doors Music Company, USA.
Rondor Music (London) Limited, 10A Parsons Green, London SW6 4TW for the United Kingdom and the Republic of Ireland.
All Rights Reserved. International Copyright Secured.

Try to set the night on fire. ____

Try to set the night on fire. __

Try to set the night on fire! ____

Organ arr. for Gtr.

Free time

Gtr.

Love Me Two Times

Words & Music by The Doors

© Copyright 1967 Doors Music Company, USA.
Rondor Music (London) Limited, 10A Parsons Green, London SW6 4TW for the United Kingdom and the Republic of Ireland.
All Rights Reserved. International Copyright Secured.

Love me two times,_ • I'm goin' a - way._

Love me one time.

Verse 2:

Do not speak._ Love me one time._

Yeah, my knees_got weak._ Love me two times_ girl,_

21

'cause I'm goin' a-way.＿　　　　　Love me two time girl,＿　　　　One for to-mor-row,

one just for to-day.＿　　　　Love me two times＿　　　I'm goin' a-way.＿

Love me two times＿　　　I'm goin' a-way.＿

Love me two times＿　I'm　　　　goin' a-way.＿＿

Strange Days

Words & Music by The Doors

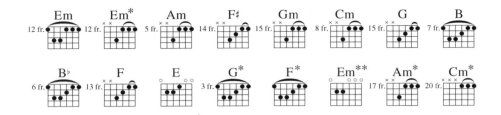

Intro

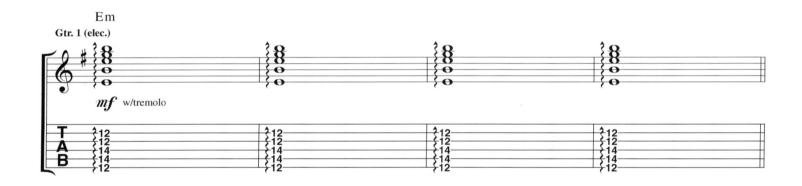

Verse

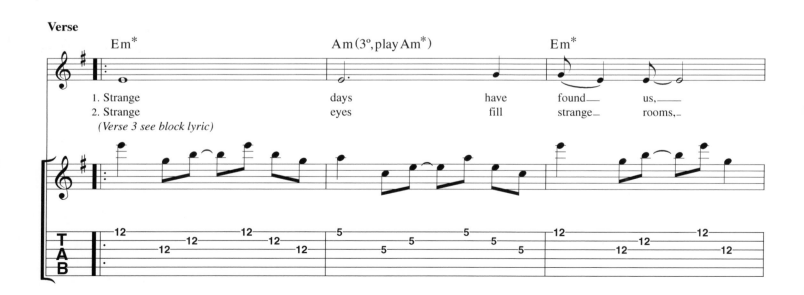

1. Strange days have found us,
2. Strange eyes fill strange rooms,

(Verse 3 see block lyric)

© Copyright 1967 Doors Music Company, USA.
Rondor Music (London) Limited, 10A Parsons Green, London SW6 4TW for the United Kingdom and the Republic of Ireland.
All Rights Reserved. International Copyright Secured.

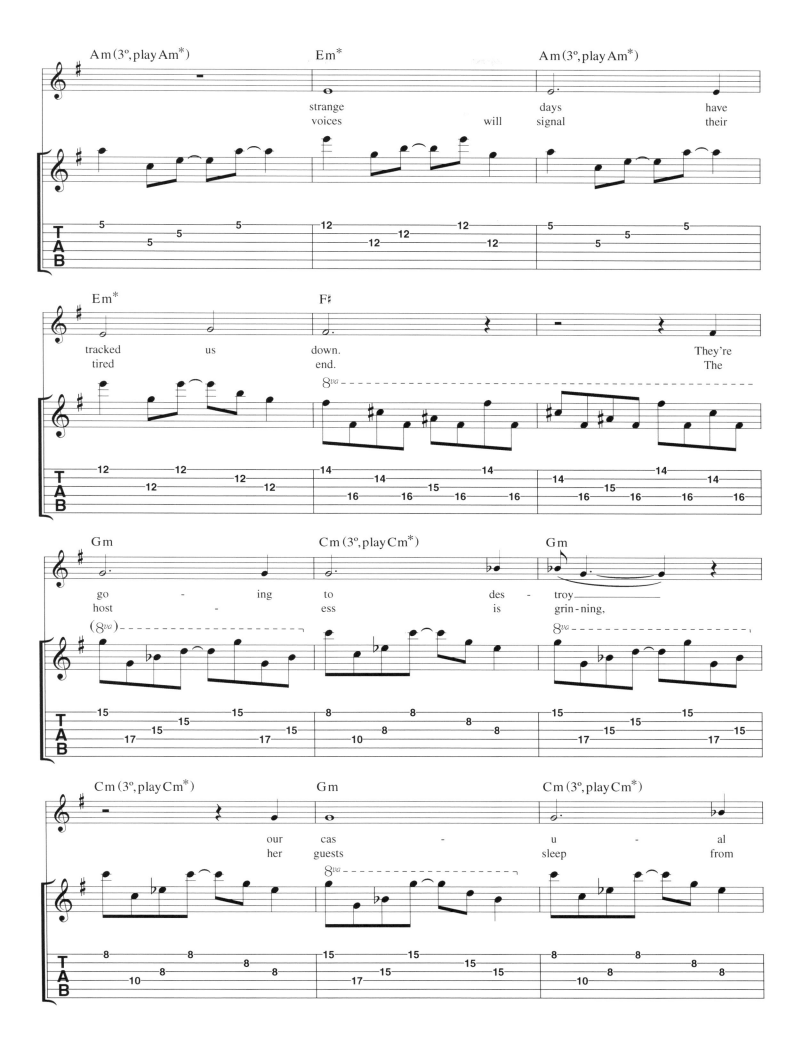

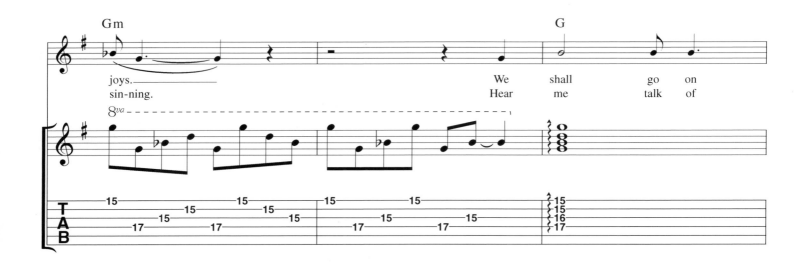

joys. _____

sin-ning.   We   shall   go   on

                                             Hear   me   talk   of

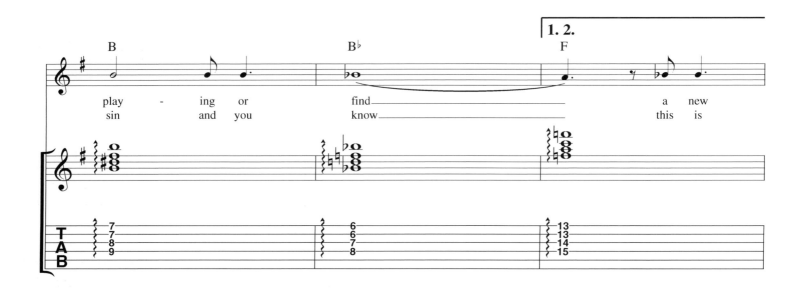

play - ing   or   find _____ a   new

sin   and you   know _____ this   is

1. 2.

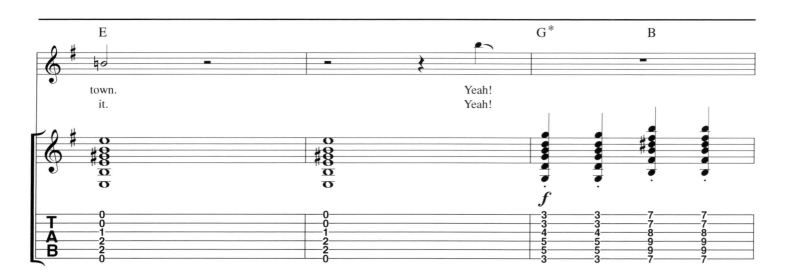

town.   Yeah!

it.   Yeah!

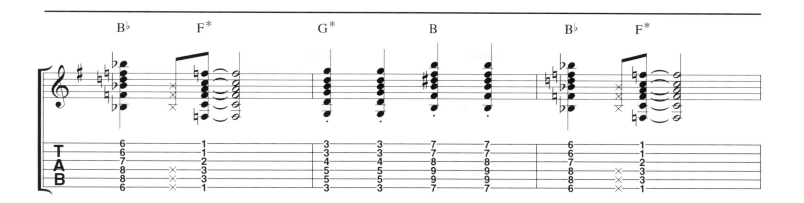

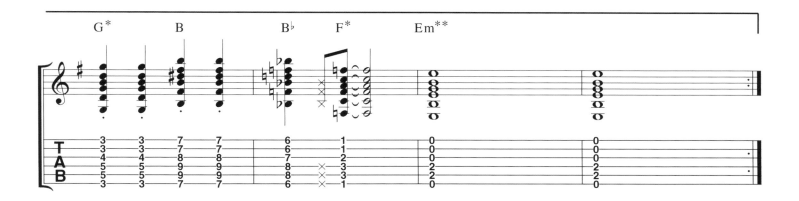

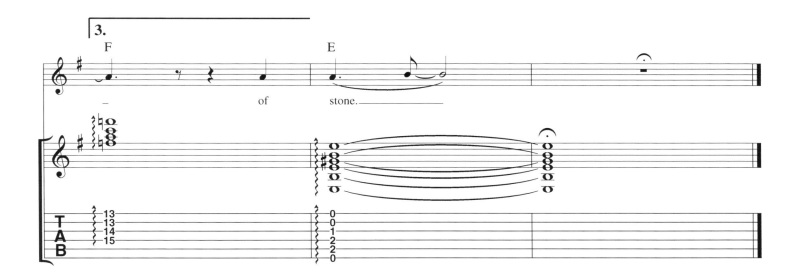

Verse 3:

Strange days have found us
And through their strange hours
We linger alone
Bodies confused
Memories misused
As we run from the day
To a strange night of stone

Roadhouse Blues

Words & Music by The Doors

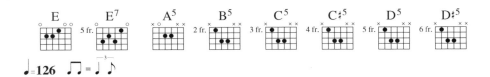

Intro

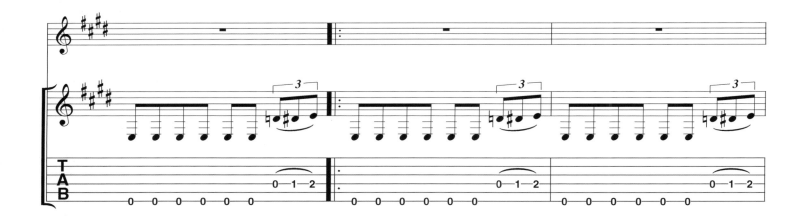

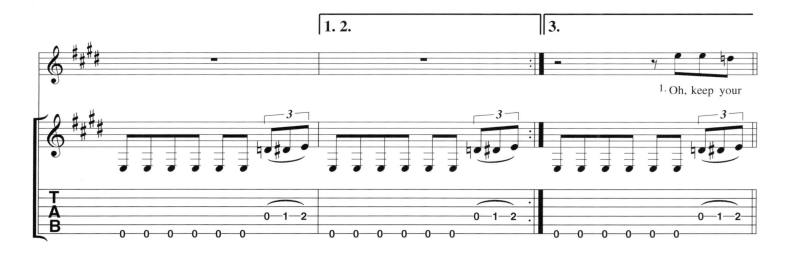

© Copyright 1970 Doors Music Company, USA.
Rondor Music (London) Limited, 10A Parsons Green, London SW6 4TW for the United Kingdom and the Republic of Ireland.
All Rights Reserved. International Copyright Secured.

Chorus

eyes on the road, your hands___ up - on___ the wheel.___

Oh, keep your eyes on the road, your hands___ up - on___ the wheel.-

Come to the road - house

gon - na have a real,___ a good time.___

29

back at the road-house they got some bun-ga-lows,—
3. (%) woke up this morn - ing I got my-self a beer,—

and a back at the road - house they got some bun - ga - lows,—
well I woke up this morn - ing, I got my - self a beer,—

30

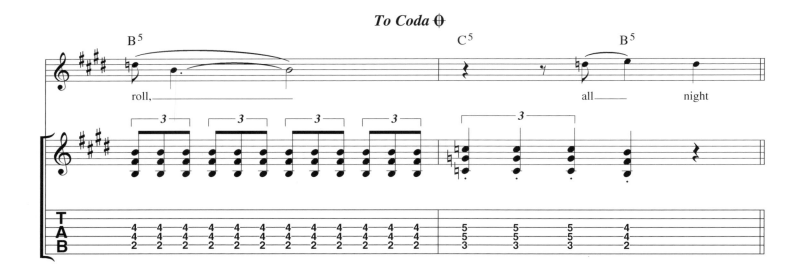

Solo

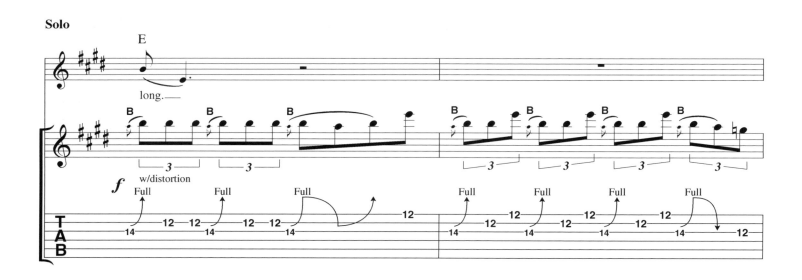

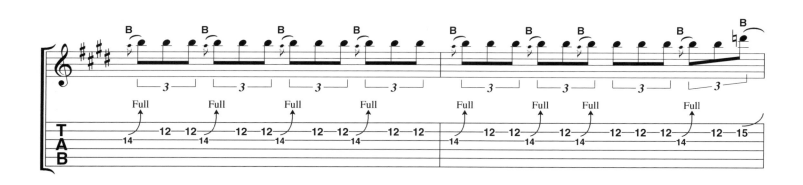

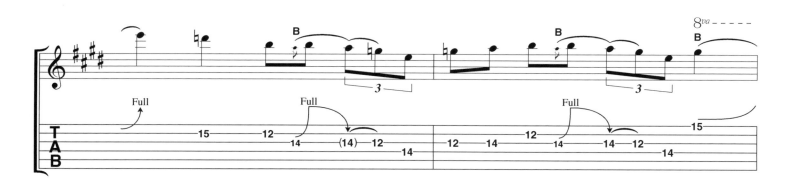

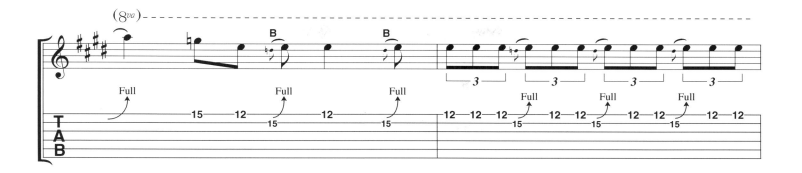

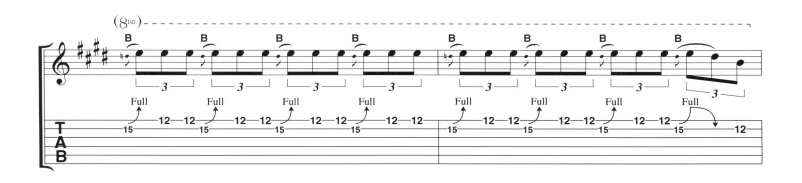

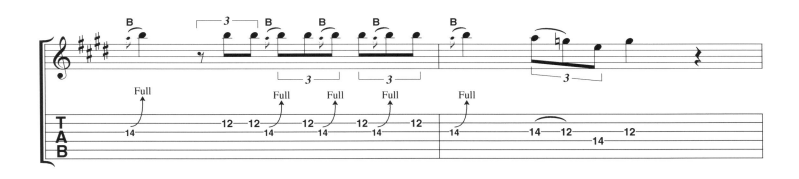

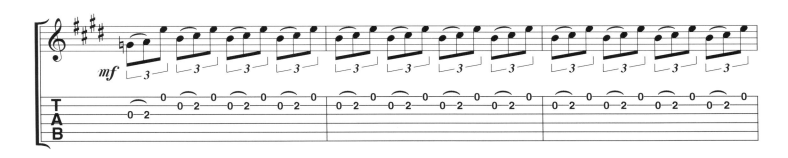

33

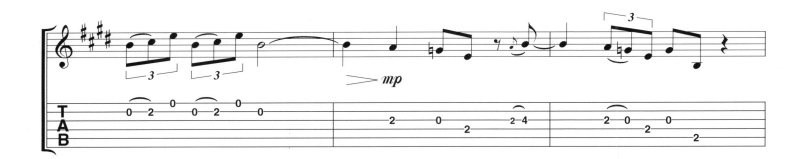

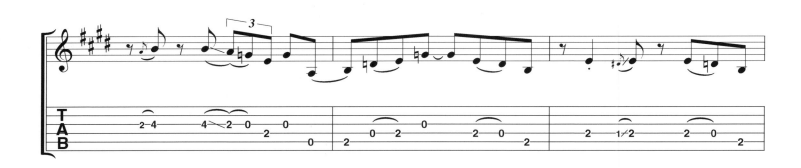

You got - ta

roll, roll, roll, got - ta thrill my soul,————— oh, gon - na win you,

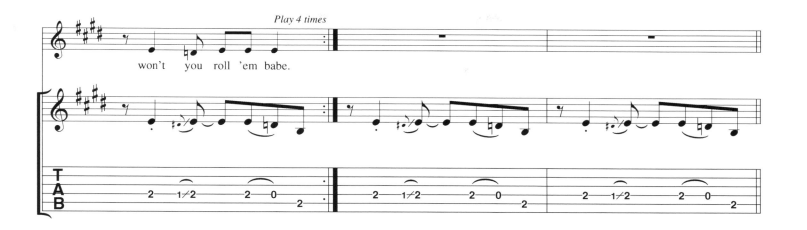

won't you roll 'em babe.

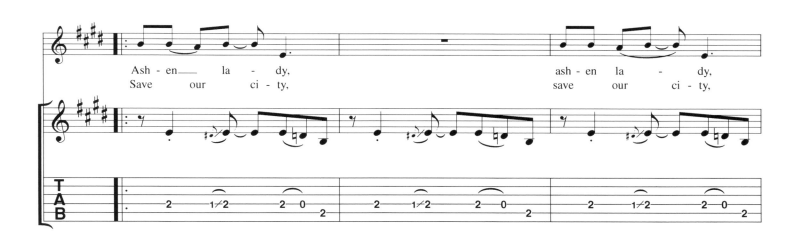

Ash - en —— la - dy,   ash - en la - dy,
Save   our   ci - ty,   save   our   ci - ty,

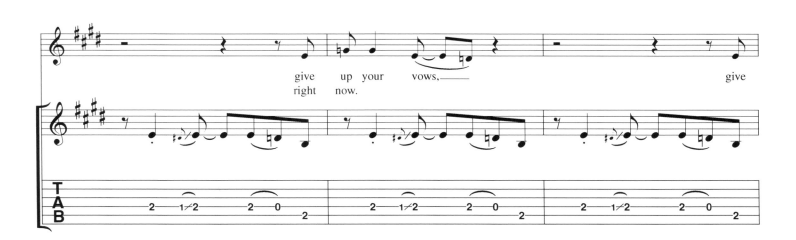

give   up your   vows,——   give
right   now.

up your vows.———

1.

2.

E⁷

D.%. al Coda

3. Yeah and I

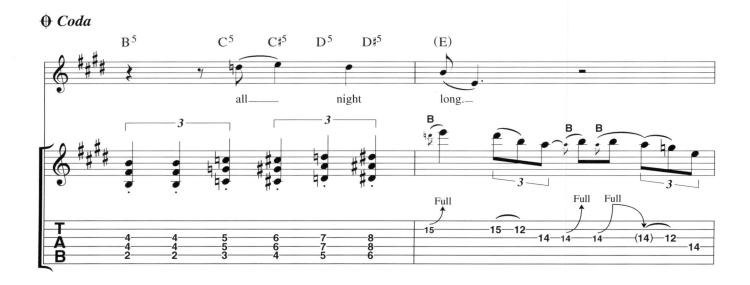

⊕ *Coda*

B⁵   C⁵   C♯⁵   D⁵   D♯⁵   (E)

all——— night long.———

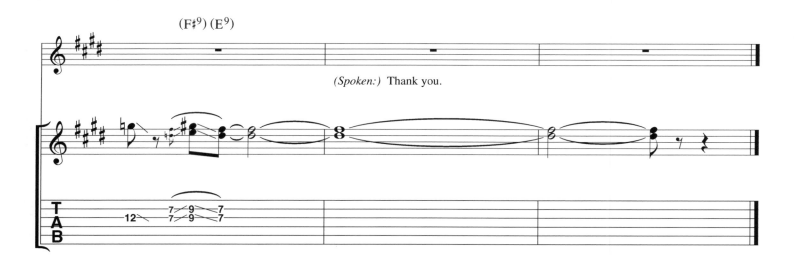

(F♯⁹) (E⁹)

(Spoken:) Thank you.

36

Break On Through (To The Other Side)

Words & Music by The Doors

© Copyright 1967 Doors Music Company, USA.

Rondor Music (London) Limited, 10A Parsons Green, London SW6 4TW for the United Kingdom and the Republic of Ireland.
All Rights Reserved. International Copyright Secured.

Break on   through.___   Break on   through.___   Break on   through.___

Break on   through.___   Yeah,   yeah,   yeah,   yeah,

yeah,   yeah,   yeah,   yeah,   yeah.

Verse 3:
I found an island in your heart,
A country in your eyes.
Arms that chain, eyes that lie.

Moonlight Drive

Words & Music by The Doors

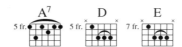

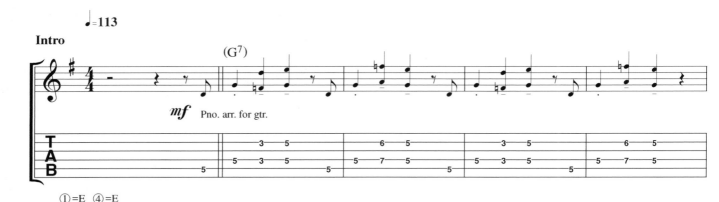

Intro

mf Pno. arr. for gtr.

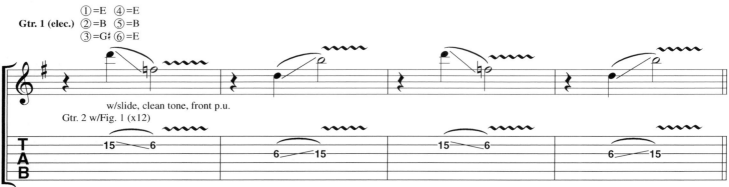

Gtr. 1 (elec.)
①=E ④=E
②=B ⑤=B
③=G♯ ⑥=E

w/slide, clean tone, front p.u.
Gtr. 2 w/Fig. 1 (x12)

Verse

1. Let's swim to the moon,— uh huh, let's climb through the tide.

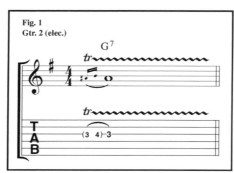

Fig. 1
Gtr. 2 (elec.)

© Copyright 1967 Doors Music Company, USA.
Rondor Music (London) Limited, 10A Parsons Green, London SW6 4TW for the United Kingdom and the Republic of Ireland.
All Rights Reserved. International Copyright Secured.

42

moon - light_____ drive._____

Switch to bridge p.u.

Solo

† heavy slide + vib. (notes approx.)

Switch to front p.u.

44

Alabama Song (Whiskey Bar)

Words by Bertolt Brecht. Music by Kurt Weill

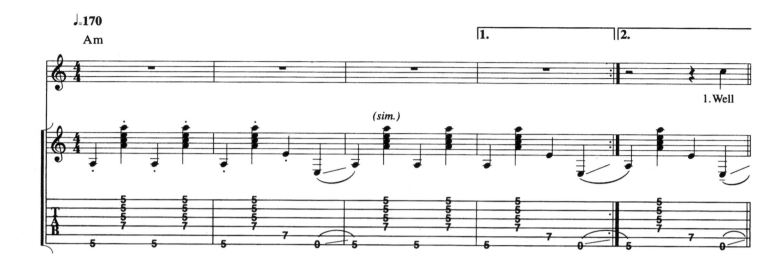

* On 𝄋 the first 4 bars of verse 2 are A major

© Copyright 1931 Universal Edition.
Reproduced by permission of Alfred A. Kalmus Limited.
All Rights Reserved. International Copyright Secured.

now   must say good - bye,_____ we've_ lost   our good old__

_ ma - ma   and   must have whis-key oh_ you know why._____ Oh,

moon   of A - la - ba - - - - ma,   and now

must say good - bye._____ We've_ lost   our   good old

hold _ _ _ _ _ _ _ _ sim.

Five To One

Words & Music by The Doors

© Copyright 1968 Doors Music Company, USA.
Rondor Music (London) Limited, 10A Parsons Green, London SW6 4TW for the United Kingdom and the Republic of Ireland.
All Rights Reserved. International Copyright Secured.

may take long - er.___ They got the guns___ but___ we got the num - bers.___

Gon - na win___ yeah, we're tak - in' o - ver. Come on!

Guitar solo

Verse 3:
N.C.

Your ball-room days are ov - er ba - by. Night___ is draw-ing near.___

Shad - ows___ of the ev - 'ning___ crawl a - cross the years.___

You walk a - cross the floor___ wit da___ flow - er in your hand;___ Try-'na tell me no - one___

un - der - stands.___ Trade in your ho - urs for a hand - ful of dimes.___

Gon - na make it, ba - by, in our prime.___ Get to - geth - er one more time.___

Get to - geth - er one more time.___ Get to - geth - er one more time.___

Get to - geth - er one more time.___ Get to - geth - er

one more time.___ Get to - geth - er one more___ time.___

*Lead vocal ad lib. on "Get together one more time."

Spoken: "Hey come on honey, you go along home and wait for me baby, I'll be there in just a

little while. You see, I got to go out in this car with these people..."

Get to - geth - er   one more   time. _____

Get to - geth - er one more time. _____ Get to - geth - er got - ta

get to - geth - er got - ta get to - geth - er got - ta.

Spoken: "Take you up in the mountains and... ha, ha, ha. I love my girl.

She's lookin' good, lookin' real beautiful. I love ya, come on..."

Love Her Madly

Words & Music by The Doors

© Copyright 1971 Doors Music Company, USA.
Rondor Music (London) Limited, 10A Parsons Green, London SW6 4TW for the United Kingdom and the Republic of Ireland.
All Rights Reserved. International Copyright Secured.

love is___ gone,___ so sing a lone - ly song___ of a

deep blue dream.___ Sev - en hor - ses__ seem, to be on the

mark.

___ don't you love__ her?_____ Don't you

love her as ___ she's walk - ing out__ the door?___

mark.

Touch Me

Words & Music by The Doors

© Copyright 1968 Doors Music Company, USA.
Rondor Music (London) Limited, 10A Parsons Green, London SW6 4TW for the United Kingdom and the Republic of Ireland.
All Rights Reserved. International Copyright Secured.

Back Door Man

Words & Music by Willie Dixon

© Copyright 1969 Hoochie Coochie Music/Arc Music Corporation, USA.
Bug Music Limited, 31 Milson Road, London W14 0LJ (70%)/Jewel Music Publishing Company Limited, 22 Denmark Street, London WC2H 8NA (30%).
All Rights Reserved. International Copyright Secured.

I'm a back door— man,   the

men don't— know,— but the lit-tle girls— un-der-stand.—

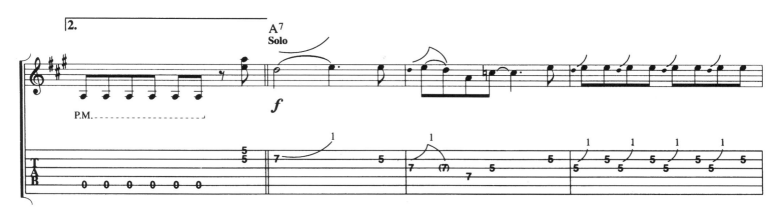

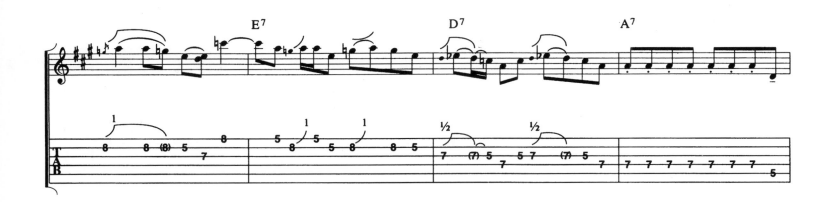

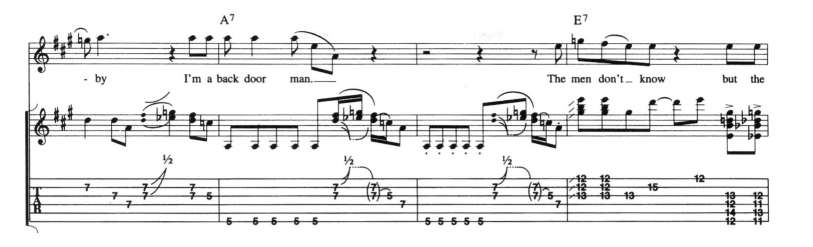

-by   I'm a back door   man.____   The men don't_ know   but the

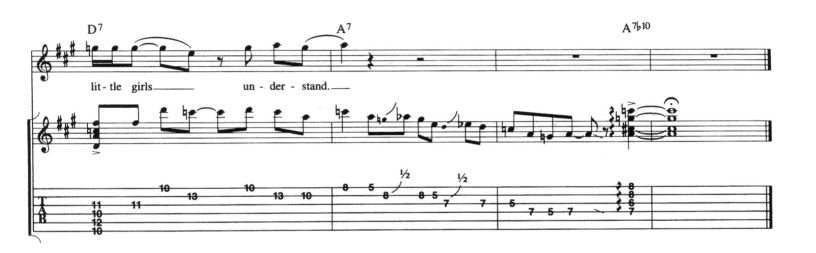

lit - tle girls_____   un - der - stand.___

Verse 2:
Hey all you people there tryin' to sleep
I'm out to make it with my midnight treat
Yeah, took down the back door man
The men don't know but the little girls understand.

Verse 3 (𝄋):
You men eat your dinner, eat your poor canned beans
I eat more chicken than a man ever seen, yeah, yeah
I'm a back door man
The men don't know but the little girls understand.

People Are Strange

Words & Music by The Doors

© Copyright 1967 Doors Music Company, USA.
Rondor Music (London) Limited, 10A Parsons Green, London SW6 4TW for the United Kingdom and the Republic of Ireland.
All Rights Reserved. International Copyright Secured.

The Unknown Soldier

Words & Music by The Doors

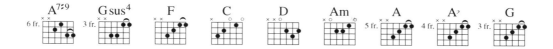

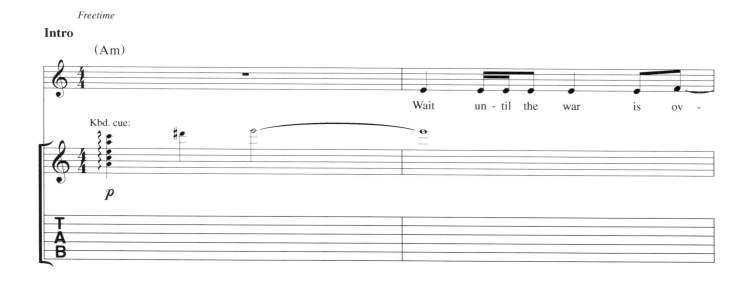

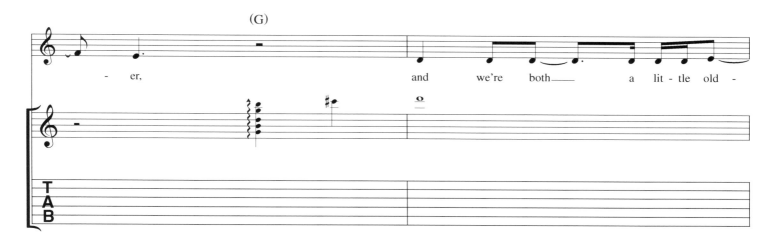

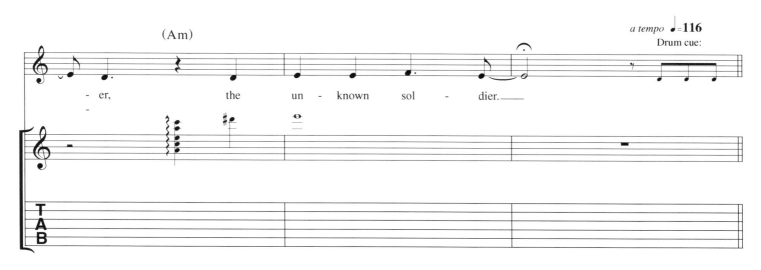

© Copyright 1968 Doors Music Company, USA.
Rondor Music (London) Limited, 10A Parsons Green, London SW6 4TW for the United Kingdom and the Republic of Ireland.
All Rights Reserved. International Copyright Secured.

Verse

72

Chorus

it's all ov - er for the un-known sol -
it's all ov - er, the war is ov -

To Coda ⊕

- dier. It's all ov - er for the
- er. It's all ov - er.

un - known sol - dier. Ah.

One, two, one, two, three, four.

Snare cue:

One, two, one, two, three, four.

2.

Freetime

Halt! *Present, arms!*

Drum roll:

SFX shot:

w/SFX of rifles cocking

Freetime

(Am)

Make a grave___ for the un - known sol -

Kbd. cue:

mp

(G)

- dier, nest - led in your hol - low shoul -

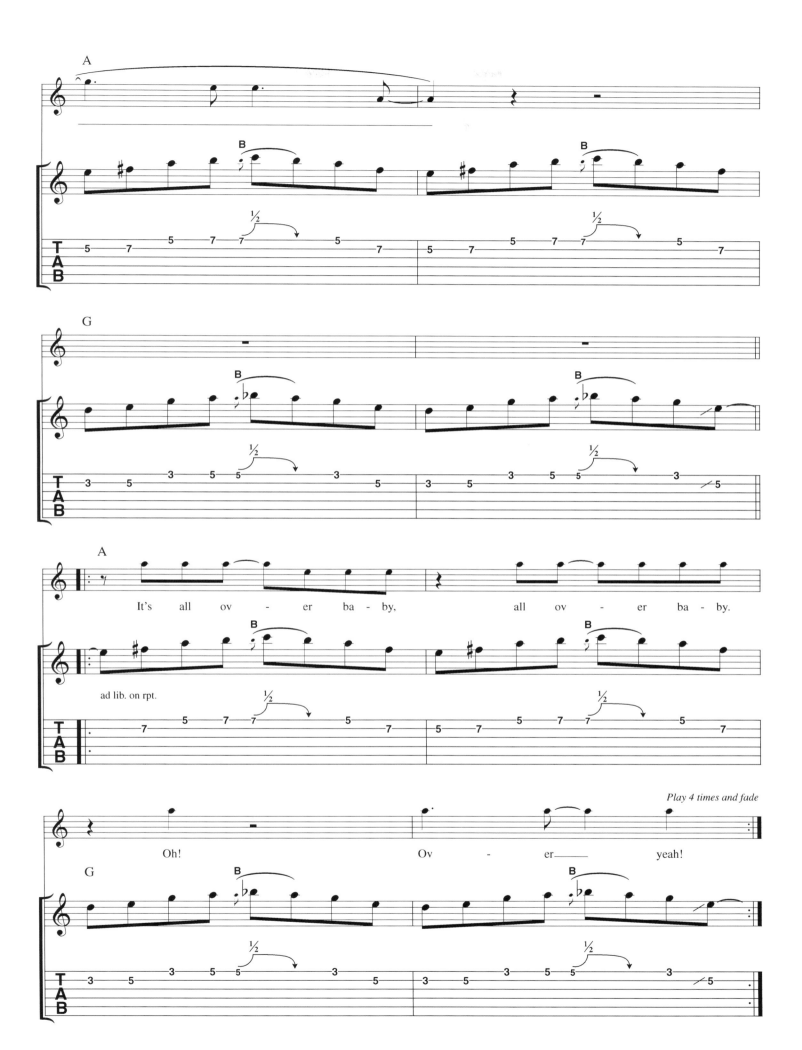

L.A. Woman

Words & Music by The Doors

© Copyright 1971 Doors Music Company, USA.
Rondor Music (London) Limited, 10A Parsons Green, London SW6 4TW for the United Kingdom and the Republic of Ireland.
All Rights Reserved. International Copyright Secured.

Verse 1:
w/Rhy. Fig. 1 *(4½ times)*

Well I just got in-to town a-bout an ho-ur a-go._

I took a look a-round see which way the wind_blows.

With a lit-tle girl in a Hol-ly-wood bun-ga-low._

Are you a luck-y lit-tle la-dy in the cit-y of light?_

Or just an-oth-er lost an-gel?___ Cit-y of night,_____ cit-y of night._

Cit-y of night,_ cit-y of night._ Whoa! Come on!

Guitar solo
w/Rhy. Fig. 1 *(6 times)*

Rhy. Fig. 2 (Gtr. II) -

Verse 2:
w/Rhy. Fig. 1 *(4 times)*

L. A.__ wo - man,   L. A.__ wo - man.

L. A.   wo - man Sun-day af - ter-noon.__

L. A. wo - man Sun - day af - ter - noon._

L. A. wo - man Sun - day af - ter - noon,_ drive through your sub - urbs in to your

(cont. in slashes)

w/Rhy. Fig. 2 *(2 times)*
G^{II} A^{II}

blues. _____ In - to your blues. Yeah! In - to your

G^{II} A^{II}

Piano solo
w/Rhy. Fig. 1 *(4 times)*

blue, blue_ blue, in - to your blues. Oh _____ yeah!

Interlude:
Rhy. Fig. 3 - *Play 4 times*
Both gtrs.
A G A G

15

*Vocal enter last time.

So a - lone, so a - lone.___

w/Rhy. Fig. 1

Mo - tel mon - ey, mur - der mad - ness,

a - change the mood from glad___ to sad - ness.

Half time
Gtr. I (Gtr. II out)
N.C.(Am)

keep on ris - in'._____ Mis - ter Mo - jo ris - in'._____ Mis - ter

Mo - jo ris - in'_____ Mo - jo ris - in'._____ Got my

Mo - jo ris - in'._____ Mis - ter Mo - jo ris - in'._____ Got - ta

keep on ris - in'._____ Right in, right in._____ Goin' right in, right in.____

Goin' right in, right in._____ I got - ta ride in, ride in._____

♩ = 168

Gtr.
II

*C

Babe, right in, right in._____ I got - ta whoa, yeah.

*Chords derived from kybd. and bass.

Right. Oh, yeah._____

just got in-to town a-bout an hour a-go._____

Well,

Took a look a-round me which way the wind blows.

With a lit-tle girl in a Hol-ly-wood bun-ga-low.__ Are you a

luck-y lit-tle la-dy in the cit-y of light?__ Or just an-

oth-er lost an-gel?_____ Cit-y of night.__

Cit-y of night.__ Cit-y of night.__

Cit - y of night.___   *Whoa!*   *Come on!*___

L. A.   Wo - man,_____

_____   L. A.___ Wo - man._____   L. A.___ Wo - man._____

hold - *hold* -

You're my wo - man.___ My lit - tle L. A.__ Wo - man.___

Yeah, my L. A.__ Wo - man,_____ 'ay 'ay,

come on, come on. L. A. Wo - man come on.

Fade out

Hello I Love You

Words & Music by The Doors

© Copyright 1968 Doors Music Company, USA.

Rondor Music (London) Limited, 10A Parsons Green, London SW6 4TW for the United Kingdom and the Republic of Ireland.

All Rights Reserved. International Copyright Secured.

95

The End

Words & Music by The Doors

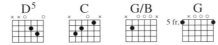

† Play strings behind nut

© Copyright 1967 Doors Music Company, USA.
Rondor Music (London) Limited, 10A Parsons Green, London SW6 4TW for the United Kingdom and the Republic of Ireland.
All Rights Reserved. International Copyright Secured.

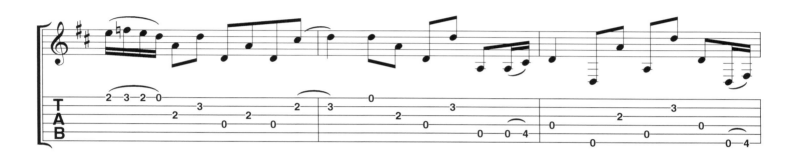

Verse

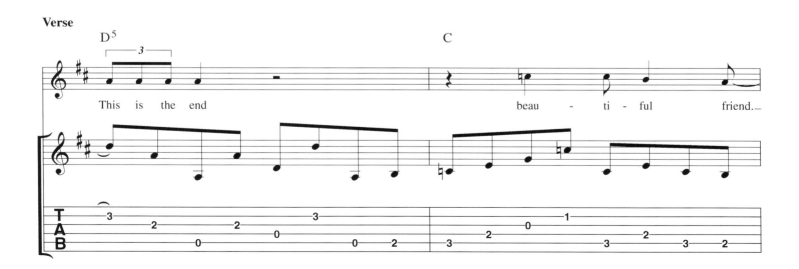

This is the end   beau - ti - ful   friend.—

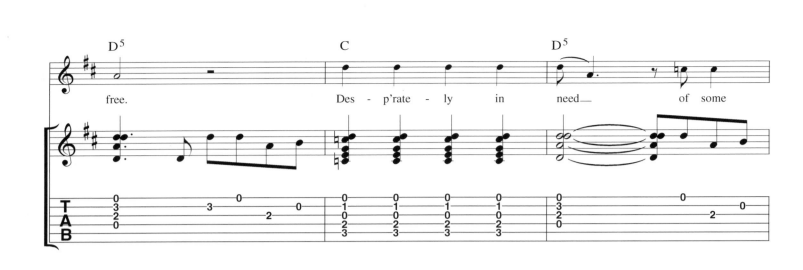

free.   Des - p'rate - ly   in   need___   of some

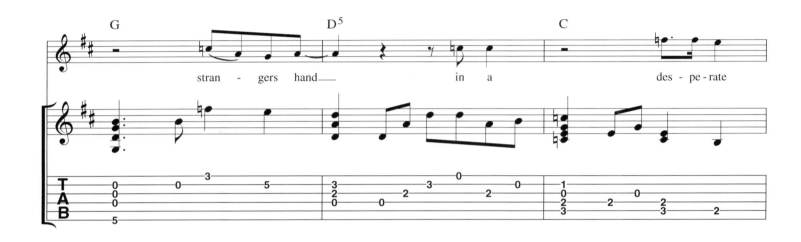

stran - gers hand___   in a   des - pe - rate

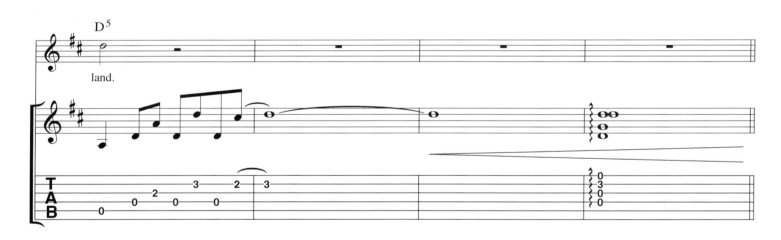

land.

Solo

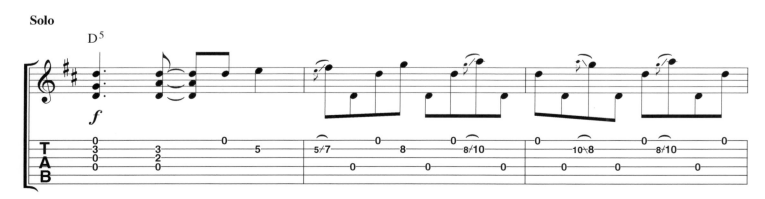

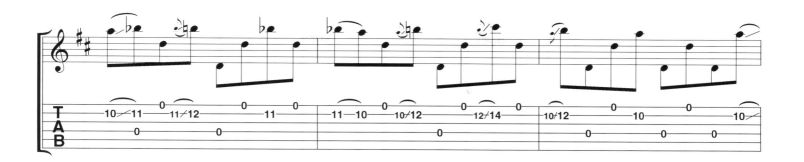

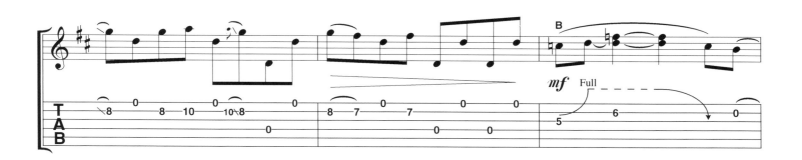

Bridge 1

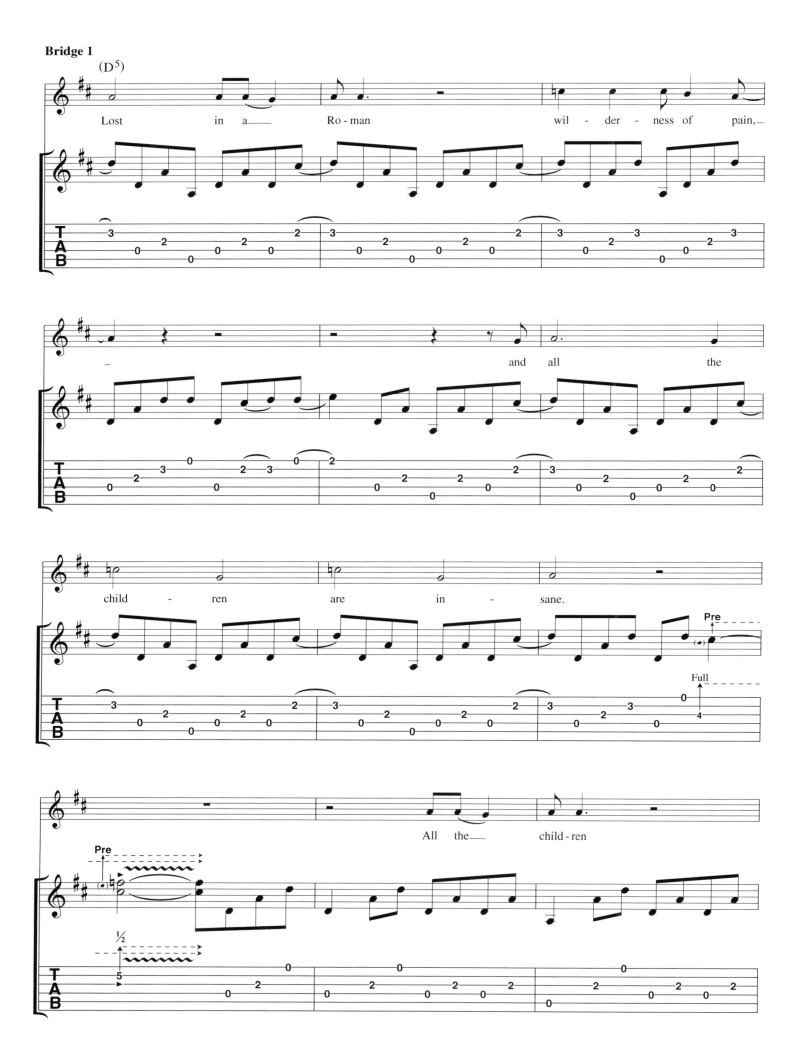

are   in - sane,   wait - ing   for   the   sum-mer   rain_____   yeah._____

are   in - sane,   wait - ing   for   the   sum-mer   rain_____   yeah._____

Bridge 2

(D5)

— dan - ger   edge of — town,—
(2-9 see block lyric)

ride   the kings   high - way   ba - by.

1. There's —

mp

1 - 7.   **8.**

cont. ad lib.

Bridge 3

(D⁵)

killer awoke before dawn, he put his boots on.
(2-3 see block lyric)

He took a face from the ancient gallery and he

1. 2. 3.

walked on down the hall.

cont. ad lib.

I want to   Mm

al - right ba - by,   come on babe.

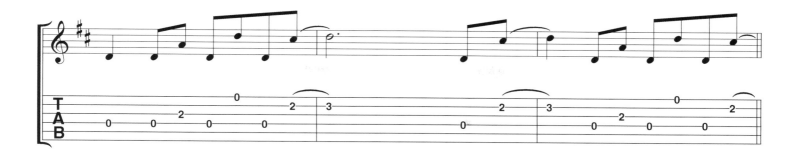

Bridge 4

1. Come on ba - by take a chance with us.——
(2-4 see block lyric)

mp

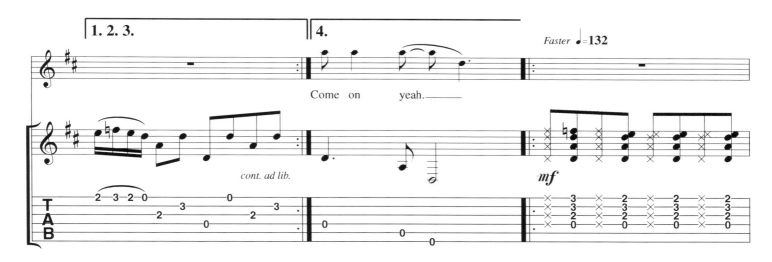

1. 2. 3. | **4.** | *Faster* ♩=**132**

Come on yeah.——

cont. ad lib.

mf

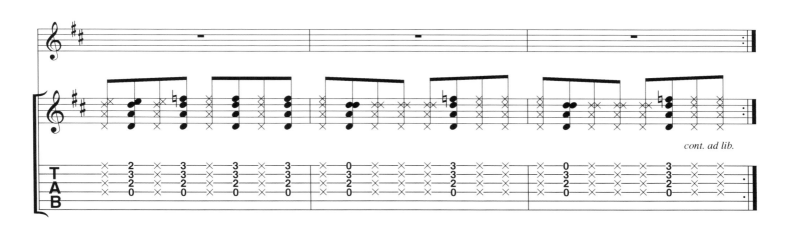

cont. ad lib.

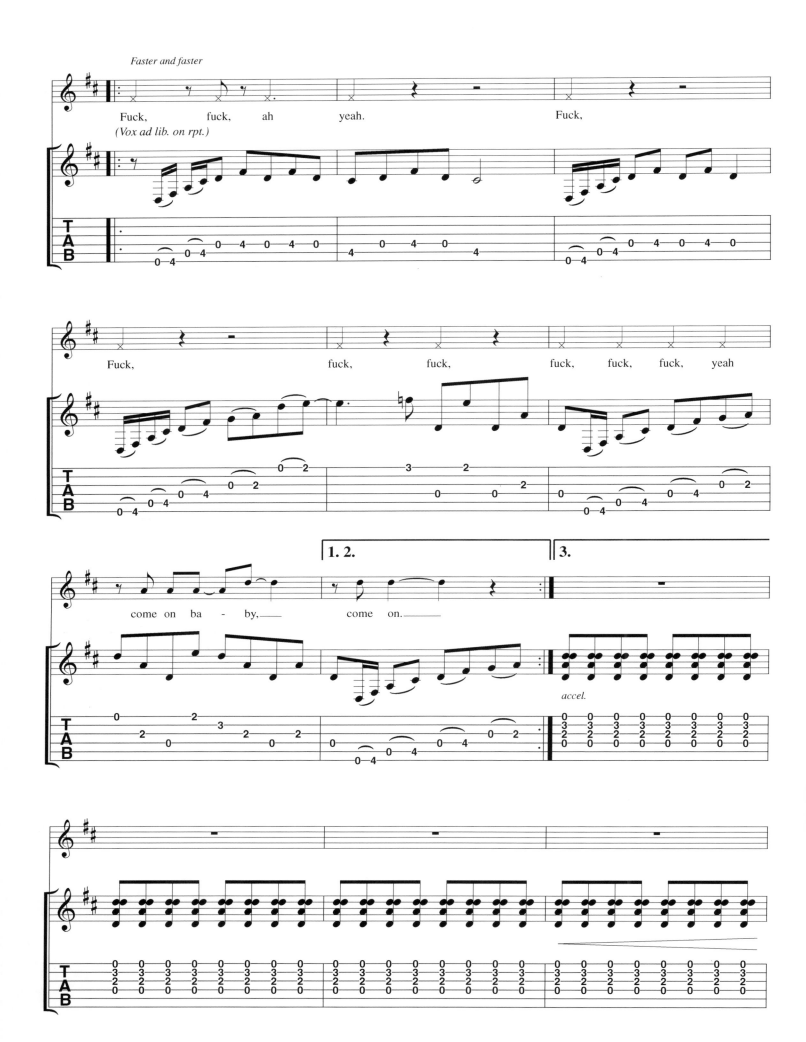

Faster and faster

Fuck,   fuck,   ah   yeah.   Fuck,
(Vox ad lib. on rpt.)

Fuck,   fuck,   fuck,   fuck,   fuck,   fuck,   yeah

1. 2.   3.

come on ba - by,____   come on.____

accel.

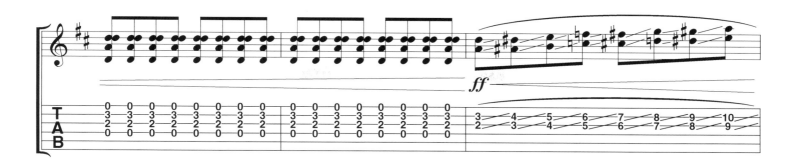

Freetime FX for 25"

(Spoken) *Kill,* *kill,* *kill,* *kill,* *kill.*

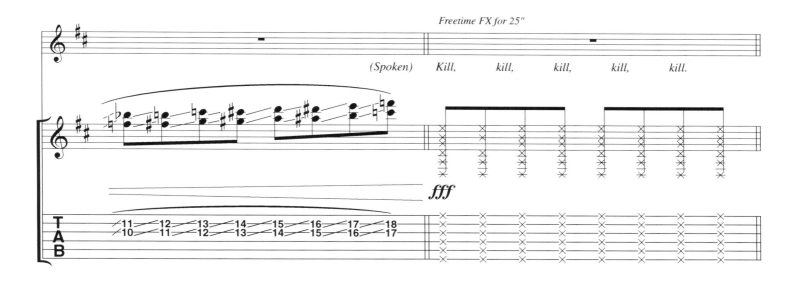

÷ Feedback

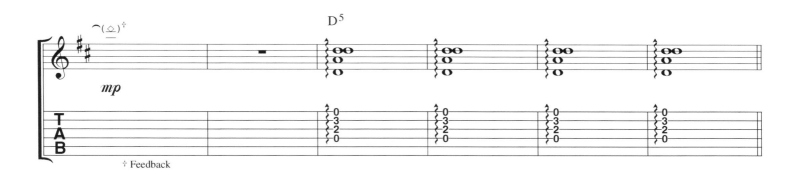

Verse

This is the end_____ beau - ti - ful friend.___

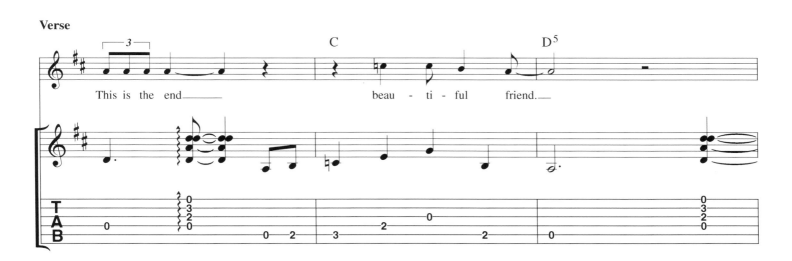

This is the end,— my on-ly friend, the end.

It hurts to set you free,— but you'll ne-ver fol-low me.—

The end of laugh-ter and soft lies.—

— lies.— The end of nights we

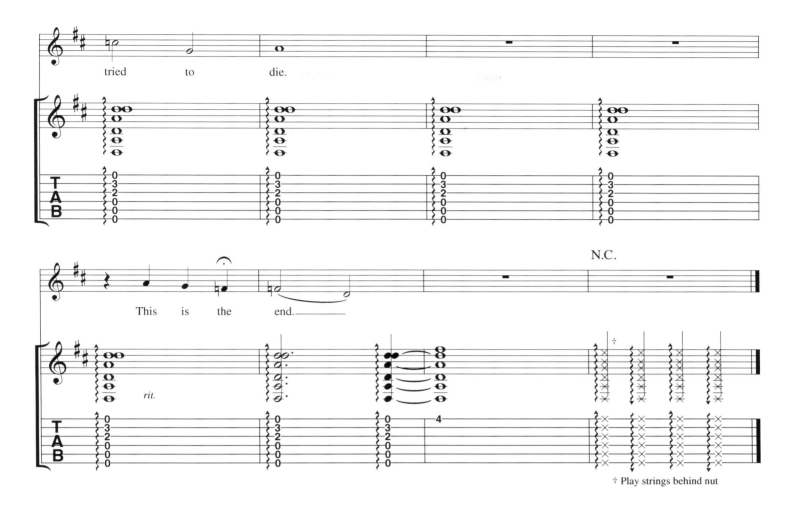

tried   to   die.

N.C.

This   is   the   end.

rit.

† Play strings behind nut

Bridge 2:

There's danger on the edge of town
Ride the King's highway, baby
Weird scenes inside the gold mine
Ride the highway west, baby
Ride the snake, ride the snake
To the lake, the ancient lake, baby
The snake is long, seven miles
Ride the snake ... he's old, and his skin is cold
The west is the best, the west is the best
Get here, and we'll do the rest
The blue bus is callin' us, the blue bus is callin' us
Driver, where you taken' us

Bridge 2:

The killer awoke before dawn, he put his boots on
He took a face from the ancient gallery
And he walked on down the hall
He went into the room where his sister lived, and ... then he
Paid a visit to his brother, and then he
He walked on down the hall, and
And he came to a door ... and he looked inside
Father, yes son, I want to kill you
Mother ... I want to ...

Bridge 2:

C'mon baby, take a chance with us (x3)
And meet me at the back of the blue bus
Doin' a blue rock, on a blue bus
Doin' a blue rock, c'mon, yeah

THE BEST OF
the doors

Contents

*G = gold; P = platinum; ( ) = the line must be played but cannot be assessed for a Medal;
non-bold type = descant/soprano recorder; bold type = treble/alto recorder.

Wistful

Brian Bonsor

© 2005 by The Associated Board of the Royal Schools of Music

AB 3137

poco rit.   a tempo

poco rit.   a tempo

rit.

rit.

Waltzing in the Air MR

Douglas Coombes

© 2005 by The Associated Board of the Royal Schools of Music

Jive Bunnies

David Gordon

© 2005 by The Associated Board of the Royal Schools of Music

AB 3137

foot tap

foot tap

The Two Vagabonds

Jonathan Leathwood

© 2005 by The Associated Board of the Royal Schools of Music

Twilight Duo

Adam Gorb

© 2005 by The Associated Board of the Royal Schools of Music

Two in One

David Gordon

Playfully ♩ = *c*.80

Player 2 starts when
player 1 reaches b. 2.

platinum
treble/alto

© 2005 by The Associated Board of the Royal Schools of Music

Nep-Tunes

Sea Songs arr. Kit Turnbull

© 2005 by The Associated Board of the Royal Schools of Music

Minuet
from Sonata in D for three flutes

Quantz arr. Sally Adams

© 2005 by The Associated Board of the Royal Schools of Music

Four on the Floor

David Gordon

© 2005 by The Associated Board of the Royal Schools of Music

AB 3137

Country Gardens

Trad. English arr. Kit Turnbull

© 2005 by The Associated Board of the Royal Schools of Music

Celandine

John McCabe

© 2005 Novello & Co. Ltd
All Rights Reserved. International Copyright Secured. Reproduced by permission.

AB 3137

Struttin' Our Stuff

Brian Bonsor

© 2005 by The Associated Board of the Royal Schools of Music

AB 3137

CODA

Melancholy Melody

Andrew Challinger

© 2005 by The Associated Board of the Royal Schools of Music

Serbian Round Dance

Trad. Serbian arr. Peter Cowdrey

© 2005 by The Associated Board of the Royal Schools of Music

AB 3137

Mr Beveridge's Maggott

from *The English Dancing Master*, 1651

Trad. English arr. Alyson Lewin

© 2005 by The Associated Board of the Royal Schools of Music

AB 3137

Cat's Tail

John McCabe

© 2005 Novello & Co. Ltd
All Rights Reserved. International Copyright Secured. Reproduced by permission.

AB 3137

Pink and Blue

Brian Bonsor

© 2005 by The Associated Board of the Royal Schools of Music

George Harrison

All Things M

All T

Bangla Desh

Beware Of Darkness

Blue Jay Way

For You Blue

Give Me Love (Give Me Peace On Earth)

Here Comes The Sun

I Me Mine

Isn't It A Pity

My Sweet Lord

Piggies

Exclusive Distributors:
Music Sales Limited
8/9 Frith Street,
London W1D 3JB, England.
Music Sales Pty Limited
120 Rothschild Avenue,
Rosebery, NSW 2018,
Australia.

Order No. AM83288
ISBN 0-7119-2523-2
This book © Copyright 1991 by Ganga Publishing BV

Unauthorised reproduction of any part of this
publication by any means including photocopying is an
infringement of copyright.

Printed and bound in the United Kingdom.

Something

His Eighteen Greatest Songs

The Art Of Dying

Think for Yourself

Wah Wah

What Is Life?

While My Guitar Gently Weeps

Your Guarantee of Quality
As publishers, we strive to produce every book to the highest
commercial standards.
The book has been carefully designed to minimise awkward page turns
and to make playing from it a real pleasure.
Particular care has been given to specifying acid-free, neutral-sized
paper which has not been chlorine bleached but produced with special
regard for the environment. Throughout, the printing and binding
have been planned to ensure a sturdy, attractive publication
which should give years of enjoyment.
If your copy fails to meet our high standards, please inform us
and we will gladly replace it.

MY SWEET LORD

Words & Music by George Harrison.
© Copyright 1970 Harrisongs Limited.
All Rights Reserved. International Copyright Secured.

3

ALL THINGS MUST PASS

Words & Music by George Harrison.
© Copyright 1970 Harrisongs Limited.
All Rights Reserved. International Copyright Secured.

ALL THOSE YEARS AGO

Words & Music by George Harrison.

© Copyright 1981 Ganga Publishing BV & Oops Publishing Limited.
All Rights Reserved. International Copyright Secured.

I'm talk-ing all a-bout how to give.

They don't act with much _hon-es - ty._____ But you point the way to the

truth when you say, All you need is love. _

Liv - ing with good and bad, _ I _ al - ways looked up to you._
Deep_ in the dark-est night, _ I _ send out a prayer to you._

all those years a - go. ___   You __ were the one __ who i -
all those years a - go. ___   You __ said it   all, __ though not

mag - ined it   all   all   those years   a - go. ___
man - y   had ears,   all   those years   a - go. _

___   You __ had con - trol __ of our   smiles and   our tears

all those years a- go. _____

BANGLA DESH

Words & Music by George Harrison.
© Copyright 1971 Harrisongs Limited.
All Rights Reserved. International Copyright Secured.

knew I had to try. Now I'm ask - ing all of you to

help us save some lives.

Moderately

Ban - gla - desh,
Ban - gla - desh,
Ban - gla - desh,

Ban - gla - desh,
Ban - gla - desh,
Ban - gla - desh,

where so
such a
now it

15

man - y____ peo - ple____ are dy - ing____ fast,____ and it sure
great dis - as - ter____ I don't un - der - stand.. But it sure
may seem____ so far____ from where we____ all are.____ It's some-thing

Dm

looks like a mess.____ I've nev - er
looks like a mess.____ I've nev - er
we can't re - ject.____ That suf -f'ring

G#7

seen such____ dis - tress.____ Now, won't____ you
known such____ dis - tress.____ Now, please____ don't
I can't____ ne - glect.____ Now, won't____ you

lend your___ hand;___ try to un - der - stand.___ Re - lieve the peo-
turn a - way.___ I wan - na hear you___ say,___ "Re - lieve the peo-
give some___ bread?___ Get the starv - ing___ fed. ___ We've got to re -

1. ple of Ban - gla - desh. ___

2. ple ___ of Ban - gla - desh." ___

D. S.% (instrumental) and fade

3. lieve Ban - gla - desh. ___

BEWARE OF DARKNESS

Words & Music by George Harrison.
© Copyright 1970 Harrisongs Limited.
All Rights Reserved. International Copyright Secured.

Watch out, ___ now. Take care. ___ Be - ware ___ of fall -
Watch out, ___ now. Take care. ___ Be - ware ___ the thoughts ___
Watch out, ___ now. Take care. ___ Be - ware ___ of soft -
Watch out, ___ now. Take care. ___ Be - ware ___ of greed -

ing swing - ers ___
___ that lin - ger, ___
shoe shuf - flers ___
y lead - ers. ___

They'll

drop - ping all____ a - round__ you. __
wind - ing up ____ in - side ____ your head.
danc - ing down __ the side - walks. __
take you where __ you should __ not go.

The pain __
The hope -
As each __
While weep-

__ that of - ten min - gles ____
less - ness ____ a - round ____ you ____
__ un - con - scious suf - f'rer ____
ing at - las ce - dars, ____

in your fin -
in the dead __
wan - ders aim -
they just want __

1.

ger - tips. _____

Be - ware _ of

dark - ness. _____

not what you __ are here for. _____

to grow, __

grow __ and __ grow. __ Be - ware __ of dark - ness.

Be - ware __ of dark - ness.

BLUE JAY WAY

Words & Music by George Harrison.
© Copyright 1967 Northern Songs.
All Rights Reserved. International Copyright Secured.

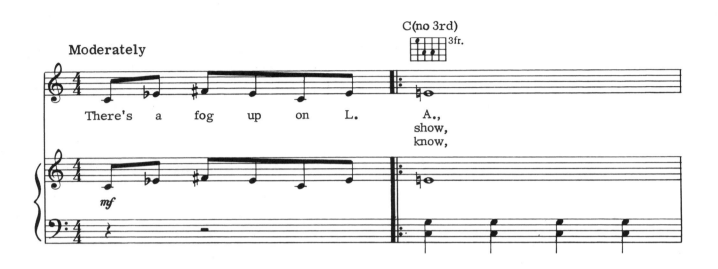

There's a fog up-on L. A.,
show,
know,

and my friends have lost their way.
and I told them where to go.
and I'd real-ly like to go.

"We'll be o-ver soon," they
Ask a p'lice-man on the
Soon will be the break of

said.
street.
day,

Now they've lost them-selves in-stead.
There's so man-y there to meet.
sit-ting here in Blue Jay Way.

A little faster

C(no 3rd)

Please don't be long. Please don't you

be ver - y long. ____ Please don't be long, ____ or

1. 2.   **Tempo I**

I may be a - sleep. ____

Well, it on - ly goes to
Now, it's past my bed, I

Repeat and fade

C(no 3rd)

3.

sleep. ____ Don't be long. Don't be long. ____

23

FOR YOU BLUE

Words & Music by George Harrison.
© Copyright 1970 Harrisongs Limited.
All Rights Reserved. International Copyright Secured.

ly, girl,   it's true.
ment I   feel blue.
___ you had to do.   I
                     I'm

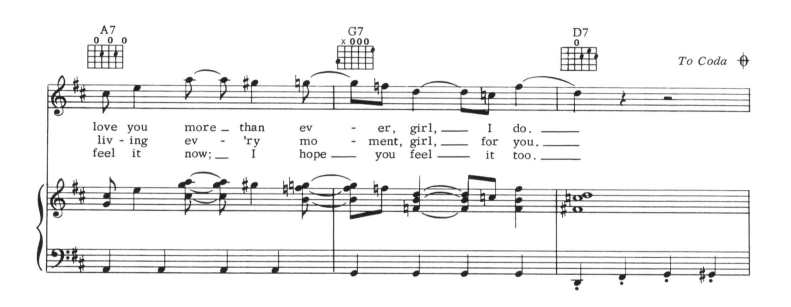

To Coda

love you more ___ than ev - er, girl, ___ I do. ___
liv - ing ev - 'ry mo - ment, girl, ___ for you. ___
feel it now; ___ I hope ___ you feel ___ it too. ___

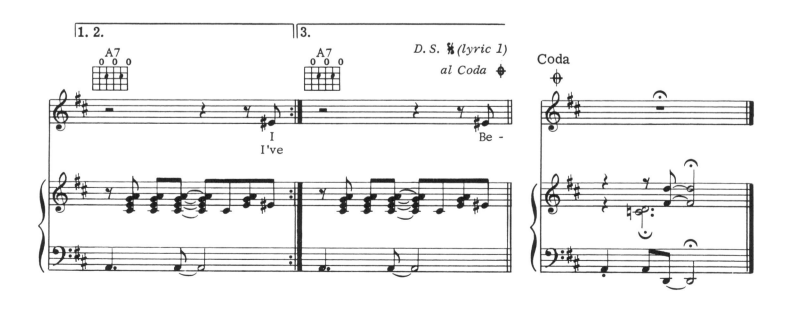

1. 2.   **3.**

D. S. % (lyric 1)
al Coda

Coda

I
I've   Be -

GIVE ME LOVE (GIVE ME PEACE ON EARTH)

Words & Music by George Harrison.
© Copyright 1973 The Material World Charitable Foundation.
All Rights Reserved. International Copyright Secured.

I ME MINE

Words & Music by George Harrison.
© Copyright 1970 Harrisongs Limited.
All Rights Reserved. International Copyright Secured.

HERE COMES THE SUN

Words & Music by George Harrison.
© Copyright 1969 Harrisongs Limited.
All Rights Reserved. International Copyright Secured.

Lit-tle dar-ling, it's been __ a long,__
Lit-tle dar-ling, the smiles__ re- turn-
Lit-tle dar-ling, I feel __ the ice __

__ cold, lone-ly win - ter.
ing to__ their fac - es.
__ is slow-ly melt - ing.

Lit-tle dar-ling, it feels__ like years__
Lit-tle dar-ling, it seems__ like years__
Lit-tle dar-ling, it seems__ like years__

__ since it's__ been here. __
__ since it's__ been here. __
__ since it's__ been clear. __

Here comes__ the sun, __ doot'n du du.

ISN'T IT A PITY

Words & Music by George Harrison.
© Copyright 1970 Harrisongs Limited.
All Rights Reserved. International Copyright Secured.

and cause each oth-er pain; how we take each oth-er's

love with-out think-ing an - y - more,

for - get-ting to give back. ___ Is-n't it a

pit -y? ___ Some things take so long, ___

To Coda

37

PIGGIES

Words & Music by George Harrison.
© Copyright 1968 Harrisongs Limited.
All Rights Reserved. International Copyright Secured.

In their sties with all their back-ing, they don't care what goes on a-round.

In their eyes_there's some-thing lack-ing.

What they need's a damn good whack-ing.

42

SOMETHING

Words & Music by George Harrison.
© Copyright 1969 Harrisongs Limited.
All Rights Reserved. International Copyright Secured.

Moderately slow

Some-thing in the way___ she moves ___
Some-where in her smile___ she knows ___
Some-thing in the way___ she knows ___

at - tracts___ me like ___ no oth - er
that I ___ don't need ___ no oth - er
and all ___ I have ___ to do is

lov - er.
lov - er.
think of her.

Some-thing in the way ___ she woos ___
Some-thing in her style ___ that shows ___
Some-thing in the things ___ she shows ___

THE ART OF DYING

Words & Music by George Harrison.
© Copyright 1970 Harrisongs Limited.
All Rights Reserved. International Copyright Secured.

47

48

Coda

Do you — be - lieve ————— me? —

gradual dim.

p

THINK FOR YOURSELF

Words & Music by George Harrison.
© Copyright 1965 Northern Songs.
All Rights Reserved. International Copyright Secured.

51

WAH WAH

Words & Music by George Harrison.
© Copyright 1970 Harrisongs Limited.
All Rights Reserved. International Copyright Secured.

wah - wah._____
wah - wah,_____
wah - wah._____

wah - wah._____

57

WHILE MY GUITAR GENTLY WEEPS

Words & Music by George Harrison.
© Copyright 1968 Harrisongs Limited.
All Rights Reserved. International Copyright Secured.

look   at__ you   all; ___   see the love ___   there.that's sleep - ing
look   at__ the world__   and I no -   tice __ it's turn - ing

no - bod-y told ____ you
you __ were di - vert - ed.

how _ to un -
You _ were per -

fold _____ your love. _
vert - ed too. ___

I don't know how _
I don't know how _

some-one con-trolled you.
you _ were in - vert - ed.

They _ bought and
No __ one a -

sold _____ you.
lert - ed you.

I
I

D. S. 𝄋 (instrumental) and fade

WHAT IS LIFE?

Words & Music by George Harrison.
© Copyright 1970 Harrisongs Limited.
All Rights Reserved. International Copyright Secured.

1/02 (42440)